W9-APG-020

THE LIVING GOSPEL

Daily Devotions for Lent 2015

Nicholas Ayo, C.S.C.

ave maria press AMP notre dame, indiana

Excerpts from the *Lectionary for Mass for Use in the Dioceses of the United States of America, second typical edition* © 2001, 1998, 1997, 1986, 1970 Confraternity of Christian Doctrine, Inc., Washington, DC. Used with permission. All rights reserved. No portion of this text may be reproduced by any means without permission in writing from the copyright owner.

© 2014 by United States Province of Priests and Brothers, Congregation of Holy Cross

All rights reserved. No part of this book may be used or reproduced in any manner whatsoever, except in the case of reprints in the context of reviews, without written permission from Ave Maria Press®, Inc., P.O. Box 428, Notre Dame, IN 46556, 1-800-282-1865.

Founded in 1865, Ave Maria Press is a ministry of the United States Province of Holy Cross.

www.avemariapress.com

Paperback: ISBN-13 978-1-59471-564-8

E-book: ISBN-13 978-1-59471-565-5

Cover image "At the Foot of the Cross" ©2012 by Jeni Butler, artworkbyjeni.wix.com.

Cover and text design by John Carson.

Printed and bound in the United States of America.

INTRODUCTION

The most spectacular miracle may be the creation of the world from nothing or the ending of the world incorporating everything. The most divine miracle may be the resurrection of Jesus from the dead and the most loving miracle the birth of Jesus of the Virgin Mary. The greatest miracle, however, is the conversion of an unloving heart into a loving heart. It is the miracle of baptism. It is the miracle of the renewal of our baptism at Easter.

The ancient world thought that there was nothing new under the sun. We were spinning our wheels, going around in circles. Day follows night follows day, round and round we go, and then round and round the sun, going absolutely nowhere. Christianity offered us a destiny, a happy ending to the story, the Promised Land after forty years in the desert, going up to Jerusalem after forty days in the desert, and our moving forward after forty days of Lent.

This booklet might help each of us do a map-check. Where are we going? Are we on the way of God? Give the Lenten discipline of prayer ten minutes a day and enter into the quiet of these devotions. We all have within us a center of stillness surrounded by silence. Stillness is pushing the "stop" button. It is the peaceful eye of the hurricane of daily life. Stillness is the centering of clay on the potter's wheel.

Silence is not empty. Silence is the fullness of God, which is diminished by noise and thoughtless speech. Be still and be quiet for a few minutes each day of this Lent—and hopefully beyond it.

The devotions of this booklet lead us from silent stillness to an opening prayer and to the gospel reading for each Lenten day. We print only a few verses from each day's reading, so you may need to buy an inexpensive

New Testament that you can mark up. Buy two copies and give one to a friend. After reading the gospel passage and reflecting briefly on it, you will be invited to act, to live with more love, but you may want to begin by contemplating what is going on within and around you. Each day offers questions for you to contemplate.

Mary sat at the feet of Jesus while Martha, serving lunch, complained. That gospel story follows the parable of the Good Samaritan, who stops to help a wounded man when everyone else goes on by. Without prayer and contemplation, we will not notice the wounded person in the ditch; we will not help them in the right way as Christ would; we will not help them for the right reason. We want to remember that what we do to others, we do to Christ himself in his mystical body on earth.

A final prayer is repeated each day. We often have a variety of petitions we make to God, which amount to saying, "take care of us all." We should remember that God knows what we need before we ask and that God loves us all more than we love ourselves. God needs no pleading. We might instead say, "Thank you for taking care of us." We know God is doing so, though we do not always see how. Sink your heart into this closing prayer each day. Let it lead you to stillness and the miracle of a loving heart.

Come, Lord Jesus.

FEBRUARY 18
ASH WEDNESDAY

BEGIN

Seek a center of stillness surrounded by silence.
God will illumine your mind and enkindle your heart.

PRAY

A clean heart create for me, O God, and a steadfast
spirit renew within me.

~Psalm 51:12

LISTEN

Read Matthew 6:1–6, 16–18.

"But when you pray, go to your inner room, close the
door, and pray to your Father in secret."

~Matthew 6:6

Dust but Stardust

"Remember you are dust and unto dust you shall
return." I like to think we are stardust. That seems to
elevate the black forehead smudge. The Bible says God
formed humanity long ago from the dirt of the earth, or,
shall we say, the good soil of the earth. Astrophysicists
tell us that stardust was formed over billions of years,
and we are the beneficiaries of those molecules made
in violent fire a very long time ago. God knows. We are
here on Earth, a planet able to support us though our
star-hearth is many million miles away. Too close to the
sun, water boils; too far away and it freezes. Our little bit of God's green earth ought to raise in us the big
questions: Who am I? What am I? Why am I? We miss
so much when we do not find time to contemplate what
is important and also beautiful. Violence in our world

has its origins in a failure to take time out and ponder the mystery of myself, of others around me, and of the God who sustains us. At the heart of it, we want to spend ourselves for others, even if the culture around us does not encourage such giving away. The Lenten season has much to say to us and ask of us. Remember we are dust, you and I.

ACT

> Today, I will consider whether I feel closer to people when I walk up with them to receive Lenten ashes or to receive Holy Communion. Let me remember throughout the day that we are brothers and sisters in need of God's grace and one another's help.

PRAY

> God, our Father,
> I believe that in giving us your Son, you have given us everything.
> I put my life in your hands.

FEBRUARY 19
THURSDAY AFTER ASH WEDNESDAY

BEGIN

Seek a center of stillness surrounded by silence.
God will illumine your mind and enkindle your heart.

PRAY

Lord, may all that I do be prompted by your grace,
sustained by your love, and guided by your wisdom.

LISTEN

Read Luke 9:22–25.

"If anyone wishes to come after me, he must deny
himself and take up his cross daily and follow me.
For whoever wishes to save his life will lose it, but
whoever loses his life for my sake will save it."

~Luke 9:23–24

Better to Give Than to Receive

We think we want to receive rather than to give, but in
truth it is better to give than to receive. Jesus wanted
with all his heart to give his life for us. "This is my body
given for you" (Lk 22:19). These words spoken at the Last
Supper can be rephrased, "This is me for you." We all
want nothing more than to give our life in love for others.
"No greater love has any man than to lay down his life
for his friend" (Jn 15:13). In our heart of hearts we seek
such self-donation in love, but we are often misled by the
selfish culture of the world that surrounds us. We find
ourselves wanting what others seem to want and tell us
we ought to want, rather than doing what, in our heart of
hearts, we were made by God to do and dearly want to
do. The "one who loses his life will save it" means that a

person who gives his or her life will receive it and give it away in love again and again. We are made in the image of God, and we claim God is love—poured out and given in sacrifice for the sake of the beloved.

ACT

Today, I will make a list of the things or situations I think necessary for my happiness and without which I cannot be happy, perhaps adding to it throughout the day. Why am I slow to give? I will take this question to prayer.

PRAY

God, our Father,
I believe that in giving us your Son, you have given us everything.
I put my life in your hands.

February 20
Friday after Ash Wednesday

BEGIN

Seek a center of stillness surrounded by silence.
God will illumine your mind and enkindle your heart.

PRAY

Have mercy on me, O God, in your goodness;
in the greatness of your compassion wipe out my
offense.

~Psalm 51:3

LISTEN

Read Matthew 9:14–15.

"The days will come when the bridegroom is taken
away from them, and then they will fast."

~Matthew 9:15

Love Grown Cold

Lent has the flavor of fasting—doing without some form
of food. We may try to say no to a habitual indulgence,
for we often use food to console ourselves or to deal
with emotional and spiritual emptiness that we cannot
overcome. If we fast from our usual diet, we may discover that eating more slowly allows us to appreciate
flavor more intensely and to recognize that often in life
less is more. We may also find our hearts learning to
love again or appreciating life anew. In the Middle Ages,
loss of fervor in living the monastic life was a problem,
and fasting became one of the hoped-for remedies in the
great monasteries of Europe. Fasting can produce in us
a similar outcome.

When we fall in love with someone, we do not pay much attention to preparing and eating three big meals a day. When in love, we have "food that one cannot see." Our attention is on the beloved who has come into our life and not on mundane things such as food or drink. When love grows cold, what are we to do? What can we do? Suppose we fast from food in an attempt to remind ourselves how love once filled our lives. That love grown cold might just warm and claim our attention again. Come, Lord Jesus! Fill my emptiness with your love.

ACT

Today, may I see food with new eyes, as health for my body and my soul.

PRAY

God, our Father,
I believe that in giving us your Son, you have given us everything.
I put my life in your hands.

February 21
Saturday after Ash Wednesday

BEGIN

Seek a center of stillness surrounded by silence.
God will illumine your mind and enkindle your heart.

PRAY

Father, you know my human frailty. Watch over me
with your provident care and protect me from sin
with the strength of your love.

LISTEN

Read Luke 5:27–32.

"Those who are healthy do not need a physician, but
the sick do. I have not come to call the righteous to
repentance but sinners."

~*Luke 5:31–32*

The Wounded Draw God's Mercy

We tend to think we need to walk up the mountain in
search of God at the top—closer to heaven and out of this
world. God, however, walks down the mountain and
into our noisy, busy marketplace in search of us. We are
his children, so lost and so endangered in the strife of this
earthly world. We are all wounded and waiting for the
medic to come and save us. It is the vulnerable child that
parents long to assist, and the child with special needs
who inspires deep compassion. It is the sinner who calls
forth mercy and forgiveness. Our sinfulness brought us
our Redeemer, the God made human and vulnerable like
us in order to save us. God writes straight with crooked
lines. We are not all called to live in a monastery or to
find a gated community of some kind that insulates us

from the poor and the disadvantaged. We are called as Christians to be God's love in the midst of the turmoil and confusion of the daily newspapers. What a happy fault that our darkness brought Jesus down to us in order to lift us up to light and life with him.

ACT

I will examine my conscience today. Do I think I am better than others? Do I find sinners are less worthy of God's love than I am? Do I really believe that, "but for the grace of God there go I"? Let me condemn the sin but never the sinner, who all the more needs my love.

PRAY

God, our Father,
I believe that in giving us your Son, you have given us everything.
I put my life in your hands.

Sunday, February 22
First Week of Lent

BEGIN

Seek a center of stillness surrounded by silence.
God will illumine your mind and enkindle your heart.

PRAY

Your ways, O Lord, make known to me; teach me
your paths.
Guide me in your truth and teach me, for you are
God my savior.

~Psalm 25:4–5

LISTEN

Read Mark 1:12–15.

The Spirit drove Jesus out into the desert, and he
remained in the desert for forty days, tempted by
Satan.

~Mark 1:12–13

Lead Us Not into Temptation

Every year, on the first Sunday of Lent, we read the story
of Jesus being tempted by the devil in the desert, where
he spent forty days after his baptism in the Jordan River.
The Church spends forty days in Lent to prepare us for
the renewal of our baptism. The first temptation in this
story is to change stones into bread, for Jesus was hungry
in the desert. It is the temptation of the poor and hungry
in distress around the world. Shall we cut moral corners
to save ourselves? The temptation of the rich and powerful also comes in the desert. All the kingdoms of the
earth shall be theirs if they knuckle under to the power
of Satan, who can cut corners to power and wealth. The

last temptation will visit Jesus again and again. Shall he call upon his Father to save him from injury and death? Shall he presume to jump off the high point of the Temple because his Father's angels will catch him, "lest he dash his foot against a stone"? He could renounce being human, poor, and helpless, and claim heavenly privilege. He could, but he does not.

ACT

I will be mindful today of my temptations. Have I cut a deal with my conscience? Do I cut corners in my moral integrity? What am I doing that I would be ashamed of doing before others? Do I need the Sacrament of Reconciliation with God and the Christian community? When will I get there?

PRAY

God, our Father,
I believe that in giving us your Son, you have given us everything.
I put my life in your hands.

Monday, February 23
First Week of Lent

BEGIN

Seek a center of stillness surrounded by silence.
God will illumine your mind and enkindle your heart.

PRAY

Saving Lord, turn my mind and heart back to you
and your Gospel. Teach me your justice and bring me
peace.

LISTEN

Read Matthew 25:31–46.

"Lord when did we see you hungry or thirsty or a
stranger or naked or ill or in prison and not minister
to your needs?" . . . "Amen, I say to you, what you
did not do for one of these least ones, you did not do
for me."

~Matthew 25:44–45

I Am You and You Are Me

Whatever good or bad we do, we do to Jesus because
we are members of his Body on Earth. Empathy and
sympathy in our lives stem from the grace of God and
from an innate sense in our bones that our lives are com-
mingled. I am you and you are me. In the account of St.
Paul's conversion, he hears a voice: "Saul, Saul, why
are you persecuting me?" We know sin hurts the sinner,
but sin also hurts those around him or her. We are in
this life together for better or for worse. The prayers of
strangers enrich us. Sins around the world deplete us.
Above all, the love of Jesus lifts us all and enables us,
because we belong to each other in our belonging to him.

The commandment "Love your neighbor as yourself" requires basic fairness in living human life. "Love one another as I have loved you," words spoken to us by Jesus in the gospel, asks more of us. The Cross remains a reminder of how much more than basic human fairness Jesus gave to us. "No greater love has any man than to lay down his life for his friend."

ACT

I will pay attention to the individuals I encounter today. If I believe Jesus is in each of them, how much difference will my belief make in whom I love or do not love?

PRAY

God, our Father,
I believe that in giving us your Son, you have given us everything.
I put my life in your hands.

BEGIN

Seek a center of stillness surrounded by silence.
God will illumine your mind and enkindle your heart.

PRAY

Father, look on me, your child, with love and compassion. Through the discipline of Lent, help me to grow in my desire for you.

LISTEN

Read Matthew 6:7–15.

"If you forgive men their transgressions, your heavenly Father will forgive you. But if you do not forgive men, neither will your Father forgive your transgressions."

~Matthew 6:14–15

Catch the Ball before You Throw It

Forgiveness is never earned, but only freely given. Love is never earned but only freely given. To forgive, you must first be forgiven, though you may not know it. To love, you must first be loved, though again you may not be aware of the prior love. Children give only what they have received. They must first receive gifts in order to be able to give gifts, and this is true for the gift of love most of all. All of us can say with St. Paul, "What have you that you have not received?" You must first catch the ball before you can throw it. Because we are forgiven much, we are enabled to forgive. "Forgive us our trespasses [so that] we may forgive others their trespasses." We are not forgiven because we love much, but we are loved much and hence we forgive much and love more. The unnamed woman who washed the feet of Jesus with her tears and dried them with her hair did not love Jesus first and only then obtain his forgiveness. Jesus first loved her and forgave her, and she then responded to being loved and forgiven with an outpouring of her own love.

ACT

Today, I will keep in mind how much I have been loved and forgiven. I will try to hold in prayer those whom I cannot now bear. May my hardness of heart be softened by God's merciful love.

PRAY

God, our Father,
I believe that in giving us your Son, you have given us everything.
I put my life in your hands.

WEDNESDAY, FEBRUARY 25
FIRST WEEK OF LENT

BEGIN

Seek a center of stillness surrounded by silence.
God will illumine your mind and enkindle your heart.

PRAY

Have mercy on me, O God, in your goodness;
in the greatness of your compassion wipe out my
offense.

~Psalm 51:3

LISTEN

Read Luke 11:29–32.

"At the judgment the men of Nineveh will arise
with this generation and condemn it, because at the
preaching of Jonah they repented, and there is something greater than Jonah here."

~Luke 11:32

The Reluctant Prophet

Jonah sailed away from the mercy and forgiveness God
wanted him to preach, but not because he was afraid of
abuse by those to whom he came to preach God's word.
Even after his deliverance from his three-day ordeal in
the belly of the whale, Jonah was reluctant to offer any
mercy to Israel's enemy. He did not want the inhabitants
of that great city, which had invaded his homeland, to
be forgiven. Nineveh was a city so large that it mim-
icked the whole world and all the world's sins. Jonah
wanted all Ninevites punished for their sins, even children and dumb animals. Nineveh, he was determined,
was not to receive God's mercy delivered in person by

Jonah's preaching. When Jonah had total success and all the people and even the animals repented and were forgiven, Jonah pouted instead of rejoicing that salvation had come to the world.

Jesus came to preach to Jerusalem God's mercy, but that mercy did not endear him to those lording it over their own people. Jesus would become like Jonah—cast out of the city and entombed for three days as Jonah was in the whale. The gospel warns us that we can disrespect the forgiveness being offered to us in the life and death of Jesus, but just like Jonah, we cannot hide. God's tender mercy will find us.

ACT

I will read the biblical Book of Jonah sometime during this week.

PRAY

God, our Father,
I believe that in giving us your Son, you have given us everything.
I put my life in your hands.

Thursday, February 26
First Week of Lent

BEGIN

Seek a center of stillness surrounded by silence.
God will illumine your mind and enkindle your heart.

PRAY

Lord God, I can do nothing without your assistance.
Illumine my mind and enkindle my heart to do as
you desire.

LISTEN

Read Matthew 7:7–12.

"If you then, who are wicked, know how to give
good gifts to your children, how much more will
your heavenly Father give good things to those who
ask him!"

~Matthew 7:11

Always and Everywhere to Give You Thanks

Ask and you will receive. In truth, even if you do not ask
you may well receive. God knows what we need before
we do and better than we do. God wants us to flourish
and loves us more than we love ourselves or one another.
God is not a reluctant giver with whom we must plead
for the good things we need for our salvation. God does
not play hard to get. God is gracious and does not need
to be begged.

In many ways our prayer should be a simple,
"Thank you, I know you are taking care of this or that."
Many of the prefaces to the Eucharistic Prayers for Mass
begin with this recognition of God's lavish generosity:
"Father, all powerful and ever-living God, we do well

always and everywhere to give you thanks through Jesus Christ our Lord." Always and everywhere, all our days and all our ways, thank you. Your providence provides for our salvation always and everywhere. Nevertheless, *we* need to ask, for asking of another is at the heart of being human. It humbles us and helps us remember that we depend on each other. When asked how to pray, Jesus did not hesitate to teach his disciples to ask of his Father, "Give us this day our daily bread."

ACT

Do I thank God often for this human life with its many blessings? We would have been satisfied with so much less. Today, I will praise God for the good in my life. I will live in gratitude.

PRAY

God, our Father,
I believe that in giving us your Son, you have given us everything.
I put my life in your hands.

Friday, February 27
First Week of Lent

BEGIN

Seek a center of stillness surrounded by silence.
God will illumine your mind and enkindle your heart.

PRAY

Out of the depths I cry to you, O Lord;
Lord, hear my voice!
Let your ears be attentive to my voice in supplication.

~Psalm 130:1–2

LISTEN

Read Matthew 5:20–26.

"But I say to you, whoever is angry with his brother
will be liable to judgment."

~Matthew 5:22

Anger in Our Hearts Fuels Violence

So very often, the "coming attractions" in our movie theaters seem to reveal a culture fascinated with violence. Verbal and psychological violence dominates so much of our entertainment. Blood and guts fill the screen. Bomb blasts and terrifying massacres scream at us. Special effects allow us to delight in loud and explosive destruction. We are told, implicitly, that we must kill or maim our enemies. Sticks and stones really do break our bones, and names may actually hurt us. In today's gospel, Jesus warns us that angry names are able to hurt those who utter them. Our love or our hatred begins in our hearts and in our attitude toward others.

We are to love our enemies, not destroy them, even if we must at times protect ourselves from them. We are a violent and materialistic culture precisely because we do not stop to think long and deeply about the meaning of this human life. People live forever; we will see each other again after our death. And so, we must learn to love one another. Regular Lenten quiet and contemplation can bring us to the point where we will say nothing evil of another, and where we will not want to say anything hurtful, much less do anything demeaning or destructive.

ACT

> I will continue to seek a center of stillness surrounded by silence this day, stretching beyond my brief time praying this devotion. I can give at least ten minutes a day to quiet contemplation and then carry that calm with me.

PRAY

> God, our Father,
> I believe that in giving us your Son, you have given us everything.
> I put my life in your hands.

BEGIN

Seek a center of stillness surrounded by silence.
God will illumine your mind and enkindle your heart.

PRAY

God in heaven, focus my love upon you, that I may
love one another and further the Kingdom of God in
my life this day.

LISTEN

Read Matthew 5:43–48.

"But I say to you, love your enemies and pray for
those who persecute you, that you may be children of
your heavenly Father, for he makes his sun rise on the
bad and the good and causes rain to fall on the just
and the unjust."

~Matthew 5:44–45

Love as God Loves

"An eye for an eye and a tooth for a tooth," a slap for
a slap, a life for a life, suggest a tough code of getting
even with one's enemies, but no more than that. Actually, the so-called *lex talionis* systems of justice or law
that specified a punishment to match the severity of the
crime were an improvement on earlier moral codes that
led to endless feuds of escalating vengeance and cruel
massacres. Subsequently, the Old Testament command
to "love your neighbor as yourself" was a further refine-
ment of human moral behavior. It prompted willingness
in us to be fair to others and to treat them, whether right
or wrong, as we ourselves would want to be treated in

the same circumstances. The moral code of the Hebrew scriptures went that far, and it remains an advancement beyond boundless revenge.

Jesus, however, gave us a *new commandment*: "Love one another as I have loved you." That imperative suggests that we should love another even more than we love ourselves because Jesus laid down his life for us, loving each one of us, whether we were right or wrong. Such sacrificial love is humanly unsurpassable, and only the grace of God can enable us also to spend our life for others whom we love.

ACT

I will try to give others I encounter the benefit of the doubt today, and I will pray for everyone I meet who may be unhappy or who seems hostile.

PRAY

God, our Father,
I believe that in giving us your Son, you have given us everything.
I put my life in your hands.

SUNDAY, MARCH 1
SECOND WEEK OF LENT

BEGIN

Seek a center of stillness surrounded by silence.
God will illumine your mind and enkindle your heart.

PRAY

God our Father, open my heart to receive the Gospel
so that I may find my way to your peace.

LISTEN

Read Mark 9:2–10.

Then a cloud came, casting a shadow over them; from
the cloud came a voice, "This is my beloved Son.
Listen to him." Suddenly, looking around, they no
longer saw anyone but Jesus alone with them.

~Mark 9:7–8

Beloved in the Dark

Every Lent in the three-year rotation through Matthew,
Mark, and Luke, we read on the second Sunday the story
of Jesus at prayer throughout the night on Mount Tabor.
It is not a high mountain; he climbs to the top with Peter,
James, and John, his closest friends. They will be with
him when the darkness descends upon him once again
in the Garden of Gethsemane. It is the same darkness we
read about last Sunday in the temptations in the desert.
We can assume Jesus was in need of consolation from
his Father in heaven and his close companions on earth.
Things had gone so well in Galilee, but now his enemies
were gathering in Jerusalem awaiting his arrival. Jesus
was asking these questions: Where is God now in my

life? Must I go up to Jerusalem and die? Am I truly God's beloved Son?

Jesus hears encouragement on Mount Tabor: "This is my beloved Son." Now his spirits lift and he appears in glory full of determination to set his face toward his destiny in Jerusalem. We too may ask where God is in our life. Are we still God's beloved? We too will spend time climbing Mount Tabor.

ACT

Today, I will check my calendar and try to schedule a day or at least some hours apart with God to make a retreat before Lent is over. In that time away, I will seek to recognize more thoroughly how much God loves me.

PRAY

God, our Father,
I believe that in giving us your Son, you have given us everything.
I put my life in your hands.

MONDAY, MARCH 2
SECOND WEEK OF LENT

BEGIN

Seek a center of stillness surrounded by silence.
God will illumine your mind and enkindle your heart.

PRAY

Lord, do not deal with us according to our sins.

~see Psalm 103:10a

LISTEN

Read Luke 6:36–38.

"Forgive and you will be forgiven. Give and gifts will
be given to you; a good measure, packed together,
shaken down, and overflowing, will be poured into
your lap."

~Luke 6:37–38

Better to Give Than to Receive

We have many sayings that parallel the wisdom of
today's gospel. For example, "Honesty is the best pol-
icy"; "What goes around comes around"; "To have a
friend, be a friend"; "You reap in life what you sow";
and "People get the government they deserve." All
such nostrums are true, more or less. People who give
do receive—a hundred fold beyond their dreams—but
it is because God is good and not so much because we
are God-like. Whatever we give, we are taking what God
has given us and only then giving of our lives as God so
wants us to do. Other people respond to generosity with
generosity of their own. Do a favor and you will often
find a favor returned. God is never outdone in generosity, and in giving us his Son, God the Father has given

us everything. The gospel suggests we begin to practice generosity by stopping our negative behavior toward others. "Stop judging other and you will not be judged. Stop condemning and you will not be condemned." Human life is not so much a calculation of cost and benefit as it is a gift that is freely received and freely given as God gives gifts to us.

ACT

Let me never require being noticed or thanked in order to smile upon another. Today, I will do five random acts of kindness to express my gratitude for the good gifts of God.

PRAY

God, our Father,
I believe that in giving us your Son, you have given us everything.
I put my life in your hands.

TUESDAY, MARCH 3
SECOND WEEK OF LENT

BEGIN

Seek a center of stillness surrounded by silence.
God will illumine your mind and enkindle your heart.

PRAY

God of ever-faithful care, protect your Church with
your everlasting love. Remain at my side this day, for
without you, I can do nothing

LISTEN

Read Matthew 23:1–12.

"For they preach but they do not practice. They tie
up heavy burdens hard to carry and lay them on
people's shoulders, but they will not lift a finger to
move them."

~Matthew 23:3–4

Walk the Walk

In today's gospel reading, Jesus warns us about the religious leaders of his day who do not practice what they
preach. They talk the talk but they do not walk the walk.
What we say is not as crucial as what we do. That stan-
dard holds for political leaders and religious leaders. Do
not just tell us you love us; show us you love us. Words
are cheap. Deeds cost. Sweet talk, saying "Rabbi" and
"Master," is one thing, but how about lifting a hand to
lift the burdens one has imposed on others? How about
serving instead of being served? How about the needs of
others over self-interest? That question applies to us all,
because we all have impact on others and often stand in
authority over them.

We are quick to say what we believe, but a life lived according to the example of Jesus says more than words. Follow someone around for a day and you may know more about them—and about yourself—than words reveal. What do they say in private? Do they kick the dog? Action always speaks louder than words.

ACT

Have I ever thought of doing more than what is required of me? Who in my life needs a break? What can I do today to relieve the burdens of another? Today, I will do at least one thing to help.

PRAY

God, our Father,
I believe that in giving us your Son, you have given us everything.
I put my life in your hands.

WEDNESDAY, MARCH 4
SECOND WEEK OF LENT

BEGIN

Seek a center of stillness surrounded by silence.
God will illumine your mind and enkindle your heart.

PRAY

Do not abandon me, Lord. My God, do not go away
from me!
Hurry to help me, Lord, my savior.

~Psalm 38:21–22

LISTEN

Read Matthew 20:17–28.

"Just so, the Son of Man did not come to be served
but to serve and to give his life as a ransom for
many."

~Matthew 20:28

Servants, Not Masters

As children, many of us played "King of the Hill." Who
gets on top stays on top. Who lords it over others enjoys
power and prestige. We quip that our elected represen-
tatives sometimes seem more eager to protect their jobs
than the jobs of their constituents. Being served is prized
over being a server. A servant is not king of the hill. This
theme highlighted in today's gospel echoes yesterday's
gospel wisdom. It is somehow better to serve than to be
served, to give than to receive, to lose one's life than to
find it. Jesus did not come just to talk a good life; he came
to heal others and to spend his life for those he claimed
to love. In the end, Jesus would lay down his life for us.
He wanted us to know how much God loves us and

that he himself is the Father's son and the presence of the Father's love. Jesus was God-for-us. To people who wish to prove their honesty and concern we say, "Put your money where your mouth is," or, "You have to have skin in the game." Jesus gave his body and his blood, just in case we were not listening. He came not to be served but to serve unto the end.

ACT

At my dining table, I will try to anticipate who needs what and to serve them by attending to them before they ask.

PRAY

God, our Father,
I believe that in giving us your Son, you have given us everything.
I put my life in your hands.

Thursday, March 5
Second Week of Lent

BEGIN

Seek a center of stillness surrounded by silence.
God will illumine your mind and enkindle your heart.

PRAY

Merciful God, welcome me back to the fullness of
your mercy. May your Spirit make me wise and generous in love.

LISTEN

Read Luke 16:19–31.

"Lying at his door was a poor man named Lazarus,
covered with sores,
who would gladly have eaten his fill of the scraps
that fell from the rich man's table."

~Luke 16:20

The Poor Are Not the Nameless

The rich man did not see the beggar at his doorstep,
even though he was right before his eyes day after day.
If you ask, "Why do I need to pray or to attend to the
message of the Gospel?" You may need to improve your
eyesight and, with God's grace, open your heart more
fully. We all need to do that. We all see what we want to
see. We see what we are looking for. We do not see what
inconveniences or embarrasses us. That is why the poor
and needy in our midst are often unknown to us. The
poor are the nameless poor and hence of no concern and
no value to us. In the gospel story today, however, God
knows the poor man's name is Lazarus, while the rich
man is nameless. One might suggest that, in a manner

of speaking, the rich man was poor in the eyes of God. When both men die and are taken to the next life, the rich man wants to ask help of the poor man, but he cannot reach him. It is too late. Lent should be an eye-opener for each of us while it is still not too late.

ACT

Have I ever gone to a soup kitchen or a homeless shelter just to see what passes before my eyes or, even better, to lend a hand as a volunteer? Today, I will make time to schedule such a visit this Lent or Eastertime.

PRAY

God, our Father,
I believe that in giving us your Son, you have given us everything.
I put my life in your hands.

Friday, March 6
Second Week of Lent

BEGIN

Seek a center of stillness surrounded by silence.
God will illumine your mind and enkindle your heart.

PRAY

Loving Father, may my Lenten observance convert
my heart to your ways of self-giving love and bring
me to everlasting life.

LISTEN

Read Matthew 21:33–43, 45–46.

"Therefore, I say to you, the Kingdom of God will be
taken away from you and given to a people that will
produce its fruit."

~Matthew 21:43

Now Is the Time

We often do not appreciate what we have until we
have lost it. Think of the persons in your life whom you
wanted to know and love better, but never got around to
doing anything about it before they died. We may have
wanted to forgive or be forgiven by family or friends
with whom we have lost our way together. We may have
wanted to promote a good project or donate time and
treasure to a cause that would make a difference to others and which was dear to us. Now we regret that such
opportunities and such people are gone from us. We may
not appreciate our eyesight or our hearing until they
are compromised by age or sickness. We may resemble
the vineyard keepers in today's gospel. We have been
blessed with faith in the way of life that Jesus brought the

world. We may have been given resources and blessings. We may have known the grace of God prompting us, illumining our mind and enkindling our heart. Nonetheless, we may be slow to cultivate the richness we have been given until we have no more chance in this world to bear the fruit that is the love of God made manifest in this world.

ACT

I will not presume I love God as I should or could, and I will not take for granted that I have endless time to do so on this earth. If I do not make time now, when? Today, I will take one step toward healing or strengthening a relationship that I care about.

PRAY

God, our Father,
I believe that in giving us your Son, you have given us everything.
I put my life in your hands.

SATURDAY, MARCH 7
SECOND WEEK OF LENT

BEGIN

Seek a center of stillness surrounded by silence.
God will illumine your mind and enkindle your heart.

PRAY

Father of all good gifts, may I live in such a way that
the Kingdom of God on earth may draw closer to us
all.

LISTEN

Read Luke 15:1–3, 11–32.

"My son, you are here with me always, and everything I have is yours."

~Luke 15:31

The Prodigal Father

The story of the Prodigal Son is not only one of the greatest parables in the gospels, it is also one of the great
short stories in world literature. We are all in this story,
whoever we are. The Prodigal Son is ever our story and
the human story. We left our home with God, and we
are trying to get back home to him. One way to read this
gospel parable is to discover who you are in this story
of prodigal love. Maybe we are all of the characters in
the parable at one time or another in our life. Neither
son understood their prodigal-loving father. The elder
son thought he earned his father's love by obedience
and doing the work of the family farm. The younger
son thought he had irrevocably lost his father's love by
his abandonment of family and his extravagant waste
of the inheritance from his father. Both sons are wrong.

Neither son is loved because of what he does or does not do. Both sons are loved because they are the father's sons and always will be. We too, whether sinners or saints, are loved because we are God's children. He gives his love to us unconditionally.

ACT

I will read the story of the Prodigal Son slowly and in one sitting, and perhaps I will read it out loud. I will ask myself, "Who am I in this parable?"

PRAY

God, our Father,
I believe that in giving us your Son, you have given us everything.
I put my life in your hands.

SUNDAY, MARCH 8
THIRD WEEK OF LENT

BEGIN

Seek a center of stillness surrounded by silence.
God will illumine your mind and enkindle your heart.

PRAY

Lord of hosts, my King and my God! How happy I
am to dwell in your house! Forever may I praise you.

LISTEN

Read John 2:13–25.

"Destroy this temple and in three days I will raise it
up."

~John 2:19

A Temple of Living Stones

The Temple in Jerusalem was destroyed by the Romans
four decades after the death of Jesus and some years
before any of the gospels were written. Today's account
of the cleansing of the Temple from its profane and sec-
ular business must be remembered as a premonition of
the destruction of Jerusalem and the end of Temple worship ever after. Jesus would replace the Temple worship
in Jerusalem with worship in spirit and in truth. Now,
where two or three were gathered in his name, there
would the Lord God be. No longer did God dwell in a
building at a certain holy location. Now the Lord God
dwelt in the people of God.

The Christian Church is a temple made up of living
stones: the people of faith in the presence of God within
them. No longer can we corner God's presence in any
one place. God dwells now in us, his holy temple, his

holy Church. St. Paul says, "We are temples of the Holy Spirit." Here is our question today: Is our heart cluttered up with the business of the world? Do we ever set the commotion aside and enter God's presence? Lent invites us in.

ACT

Today, I will pay a visit to the temple of God in my own heart. I will take time to pray within, without words.

PRAY

God, our Father,
I believe that in giving us your Son, you have given us everything.
I put my life in your hands.

MONDAY, MARCH 9
THIRD WEEK OF LENT

BEGIN

Seek a center of stillness surrounded by silence.
God will illumine your mind and enkindle your heart.

PRAY

Merciful Lord, protect me from all that is evil. God of
mercy, free me.

LISTEN

Read Luke 4:24–30.

Jesus said to the people in the synagogue at Nazareth:
"Amen, I say to you no prophet is accepted in his
own native place."

~Luke 4:24

Who Wants to Be a Prophet?

Prophets are resented. They tell an inconvenient truth.
Prophets that we know in our own communities are
resented all the more. Where did they get all this wisdom? They were just like us. Now they tell us what
is wrong with us. No man is a hero to his valet. No
woman is a big shot in the house where her diapers were
changed every day. No prophet, says today's gospel, is
accepted in his own town and maybe not even in his
own family. When news of Jesus' radical preaching and
miracle-working reached his hometown of Nazareth, his
family went to see what was going on with him. Mark's
gospel tells us they went there to take him home because
they thought he must be out of his mind. Today's gospel from Luke tells of Jesus visiting his hometown and
speaking in the synagogue in Nazareth. When the people

heard him, "they were filled with fury" and "led him to the brow of the hill on which the town had been built, to hurl him down headlong." We resent the truth. Faith and conversion need time to grow. We are slow learners in the spiritual life. Have patience with yourself before God; have patience with friends, with children, and with all "the town" around you.

ACT

Do I concede that some of the people I live with may be saints or prophets? Do I give anyone the benefit of the doubt? Today, I will commit to listening more closely to one individual to whom I often find it hard to listen.

PRAY

God, our Father,
I believe that in giving us your Son, you have given us everything.
I put my life in your hands.

Tuesday, March 10
Third Week of Lent

BEGIN

Seek a center of stillness surrounded by silence.
God will illumine your mind and enkindle your heart.

PRAY

My Lord and my God, may the good work you have
begun in me be sustained with your faithful love.

LISTEN

Read Matthew 18:21–35.

"You wicked servant! I forgave you your entire debt
because you begged me to. Should you not have had
pity on your fellow servant, as I had pity on you?"

~Matthew 18:32–33

But for the Grace of God, There Go I

On the cross Jesus revealed the inner heart of God's
mercy and forgiveness when he said at the last, "Father,
forgive them; for they do not know what they are doing"
(Lk 23:34). We know ourselves and our own motiva-
tions so dimly. I do not believe that people are doing
the best they can, but I believe they are doing the best
that they know how to do here and now. If you balk at
forgiving someone yet again for the same offense, think
of this: They may not know how they are to live without
their sin. Deep down in our mind and heart, our sin is
not willfulness only; it is also the despair of someone
trapped in darkness, not knowing how to become free,
loved, and happy. Compassion is the touchstone of being
human. We care for our own. We feel their pain. We put
ourselves in another's shoes. In a mystical way, we are

them and they are us, and, but for the grace of God, there go I. Shakespeare said it well:

> The quality of mercy is not strained.
> It droppeth as the gentle rain from heaven
> Upon the place beneath. It is twice blest.
> It blesseth him that gives and him that takes.
>
> —*The Merchant of Venice*, IV:1

ACT

Today, I will pray to become a more compassionate person. I will pray the *Kyrie* at the beginning of Mass (Lord, have mercy . . .) with more attention this Lent.

PRAY

God, our Father,
I believe that in giving us your Son, you have given us everything.
I put my life in your hands.

Wednesday, March 11
Third Week of Lent

BEGIN

Seek a center of stillness surrounded by silence.
God will illumine your mind and enkindle your heart.

PRAY

Lord, Jesus Christ, give me life through your Gospel
and keep me united in love to all your holy people.

LISTEN

Read Matthew 5:17–19.

"Do not think that I have come to abolish the law
or the prophets. I have come not to abolish but to
fulfill."

~Matthew 5:17

Love and Do What You Will

Laws and rules have their place and we need them in
our moral life much like banks of a river, which guide
the water to find its way to the sea. A code of ethics and
moral wisdom channels our behavior toward the good.
It liberates us rather than restricts us, even if we may
feel our desires must be disciplined, and indeed they
must. St. Paul claimed we were free from the law; we
were saved by faith and by grace and not by keeping
in an external way a complex book of laws in the Bible.
Ideally, the law should free us to follow the good by not
wasting our time and energy on dead ends. St. Augustine
said, "Love and do what you will."

Love of God and love of neighbor know no bounds.
Our hands and feet may be shackled by the burden of
the law but never our hearts. "The Sabbath was made for

man, not man for the Sabbath" (Mk 2:27). Love trumps the law and the prophets for it is their fulfillment. Nonetheless, you would be a fool not to look at and take to heart the wisdom of the prophets and the experience of the community in living the Ten Commandments.

ACT

Do I exempt myself from the laws of the road when I drive? When and where else? Do I think I have done enough for love when I have kept the rules and made no trouble? Today, I will find one way to love someone better, closer to the way God loves me.

PRAY

God, our Father,
I believe that in giving us your Son, you have given us everything.
I put my life in your hands.

THURSDAY, MARCH 12
THIRD WEEK OF LENT

BEGIN

Seek a center of stillness surrounded by silence.
God will illumine your mind and enkindle your heart.

PRAY

Lord God, change my mind and heart to be like
yours, because soon I will celebrate the great mystery
of your death and resurrection with your Church
throughout the world.

LISTEN

Read Luke 11:14–23.

"But if it is by the finger of God that I drive out
demons, then the kingdom of God has come upon
you."

~Luke 11:20

The Devil Is in the Details

One third of the gospels tell of Jesus healing people.
From paralysis to leprosy, from mental illness to death
itself, Jesus touched our bodies and minds and gave us
new life. His most frequent healing was the giving of
sight to the blind. The ancient world thought that if you
were sick or afflicted you must have a demon. We still
say of strange behavior: "I wonder what got into him?"
The enemies of Jesus thought that he was in cahoots with
the Prince of Demons to cast out demons. That accusation proved to be a desperate and foolish attempt to
discredit a goodness that challenged a deep-seated envy
bordering on hatred.

Jesus was resented because he wanted to do genuine good for others and release them from bondage, whether from illness, demons, or the exploitative requirements of the religious establishment. That was the threat that generated opposition to his healing, an opposition whose motivation was not to promote the welfare of others but rather that of Jesus' critics. How often we find fault with others who are doing the good that we claim to support but we ourselves do not carry out! When others are burdened with sickness or addiction, how often do we pray for them or help them if we can, rather than assume something in them is bad or to be feared?

ACT

Today, I will try to be aware of how I respond to others who are doing good. Do I cheer them on from the sidelines, feel threatened by them, resent them, or perhaps assume they are arrogant? I will instead stop and consider in what way I might join their efforts or follow their example.

PRAY

God, our Father,
I believe that in giving us your Son, you have given us everything.
I put my life in your hands.

Friday, March 13
Third Week of Lent

BEGIN

Seek a center of stillness surrounded by silence.
God will illumine your mind and enkindle your heart.

PRAY

Merciful Father, may your love overwhelm me and
lead me to the heart of the Gospel, your son Jesus.

LISTEN

Read Mark 12:28–34.

"You shall love the Lord your God with all your
heart, with all your soul, with all your mind, and
with all your strength."

~Mark 12:30

Goodness Wins Out

Some pundits say that pornography is hard to define,
but most people say they know it when they see it. Many
people would agree it is hard to define what makes a
saint, but many of us would say we know one when
we see one. Simple goodness cannot be faked nor can it
be camouflaged. Wanting the good and only the good
is transparent. Loving God with all your heart, with all
your soul, with all your mind, and with all your strength,
and furthermore loving your neighbor as yourself, leaves
a trail of care and concern for the welfare of others,
whom you recognize as God's children. Not all the saints
talk much about God. Not all the saints are in church.
Jesus took his hat off to the man in today's gospel, who
was a man of little talk and simple goodness. "You are
not far from the kingdom of God" is an accolade from

Jesus that all of us might want to hear. When we read or watch reports of world news, we often cross over to witness believers and religions different from our own. Many of them, we might say, are "not far from the kingdom of God."

ACT

Today, I will be mindful of the thoughts that race through my mind following my interactions with others. Do I judge others harshly? How far might I be from the kingdom of God?

PRAY

God, our Father,
I believe that in giving us your Son, you have given us everything.
I put my life in your hands.

SATURDAY, MARCH 14
THIRD WEEK OF LENT

BEGIN

Seek a center of stillness surrounded by silence.
God will illumine your mind and enkindle your heart.

PRAY

Have mercy on me, O God, in your goodness;
in the greatness of your compassion wipe out my
offense.
Thoroughly wash me from my guilt and of my sin
cleanse me.

~Psalm 51:3–4

LISTEN

Read Luke 18:9–14.

But the tax collector stood off at a distance and would
not even raise his eyes to heaven but beat his breast
and prayed, "O God, be merciful to me a sinner."

~Luke 18:13

Only God Knows

One of the best reasons not to judge others is the recognition that we cannot judge even ourselves. Only God knows the human heart. All too often we put on a good show for others, but we are not fooling God. Our sins of omission are many, even if we are not always conscious of this or that deliberate unkindness. Seeking God's mercy is never a bad idea. When I was teaching, I used to tell my students often, "I do not always say what I mean; I do not always mean what I say, and what you heard is not what I said." In truth, we do not know ourselves in any depth. Only God sees the depths of our heart. If I think I belong in the first row, let me not presume. I may talk a better talk than I walk. If I think I belong in the last row, let me not despair. God knows. I may walk a better walk than I talk. God knows. This gospel passage may just explain why Catholics on Sunday morning tend to fill up the back pews, and let us not think badly of anyone who sits in the front pew. Only God knows.

ACT

> I will carve out fifteen or twenty minutes today to sit quietly and examine the state of my soul. Do I think I am not like the rest of humanity? Do I feel as though I hide my truest self? What can I do to change?

PRAY

> God, our Father,
> I believe that in giving us your Son, you have given us everything.
> I put my life in your hands.

SUNDAY, MARCH 15
FOURTH WEEK OF LENT

BEGIN

Seek a center of stillness surrounded by silence.
God will illumine your mind and enkindle your heart.

PRAY

Father of peace, I have known your son, my Lord
Jesus Christ, in his forgiveness. May the Easter
mystery deepen my faith, hope, and love so that I live
praising you in all I do.

LISTEN

Read John 3:14–21.

For God so loved the world that he gave his only
Son, so that everyone who believes in him might not
perish but might have eternal life.

~John 3:16

Everyone Who Believes

We see, "for God so loved the world that he gave his only
Son" in many places, from billboards on the highway to
signs in the ballpark. It is a succinct summary of the Gospel. God came to save all of humanity. "For God did not
send his Son into the world to condemn the world, but
that the world might be saved through him" (Jn 3:17). It
is hard to add to this generosity of God, and we know
that God is infinitely resourceful. The idea that what God
wants God gets is not a stretch of our imagination. God's
sovereign providence overshadows us, and God truly
does have the whole world in his hands. Jesus spoke
these words to Nicodemus, a Pharisee who came to Jesus
at night and in secret, but he came, unlike many of the

Pharisees who claimed to know something of God and found Jesus in the way. Nicodemus came again after Jesus had died on the cross, and he provided Jesus a decent burial. He was a good man who was nibbling on the edges, slow to believe, reluctant to commit himself to following Jesus. There is a lot of Nicodemus in all of us.

ACT

I will be mindful of where I sit in church on Sunday mornings. What does this say about how I experience worship and what sort of follower of Jesus I am? Do I hide, hoping no one will interact with me, or am I bold about my discipleship? Perhaps I will change my seat.

PRAY

God, our Father,
I believe that in giving us your Son, you have given us everything.
I put my life in your hands.

Monday, March 16
Fourth Week of Lent

BEGIN

Seek a center of stillness surrounded by silence.
God will illumine your mind and enkindle your heart.

PRAY

Hear, O Lord, and have pity on me: O Lord, be my
helper.
You changed my mourning into dancing;
O Lord, my God, forever will I give you thanks."

~Psalm 30:11–12a, 13b

LISTEN

Read John 4:43–54.

"Sir, come down before my child dies." Jesus said to
him, "You may go; your son will live."

~John 4:49–50

Say but the Word

When we are about to receive Holy Communion we echo
the gospel words of a Roman centurion spoken to Jesus:
"Lord, I am not worthy that you should come under
my roof, but only say the word, and my soul shall be
healed." Jesus marveled at the man's faith. We marvel
at a hands-off, long-distance miracle worked by only the
verbal promise of Jesus. Today's gospel may well be a
variant of the same story, or yet another long-distance
miracle.

We touch on a miracle quite often. It is not long-
distance. We receive the Lord in Holy Communion,
when he comes as close to us as possible. Nevertheless,
what we receive depends on the faith and willingness

we bring to the altar, even as our faith and willingness are bolstered by this gift of grace that is the Lord Jesus himself. "This is my body given for you" means simply "This is me for you." Jesus told his disciples that he had not found such faith as he saw in this Roman centurion who trusted that Jesus could do what could not be seen. Might we not promote that same hopefulness and willingness in ourselves so that we might receive the miracle healing of the soul that Jesus came to bring everyone?

ACT

Let me resolve to say the words before Holy Communion with new-found faith that Jesus can also reach deeply into my heart and into my life. Today, this will be my mantra: Lord, I believe, help my unbelief.

PRAY

God, our Father,
I believe that in giving us your Son, you have given us everything.
I put my life in your hands.

Tuesday, March 17
Fourth Week of Lent

BEGIN

Seek a center of stillness surrounded by silence.
God will illumine your mind and enkindle your heart.

PRAY

All you who are thirsty, come to the water!
You who have no money, come, buy grain and eat;
Come, buy grain without money, wine and milk
without cost!
Pay attention and come to me; listen, that you may
have life.

~Isaiah 55:1, 3a

LISTEN

Read John 5:1–16.

"Sir, I have no one to put me into the pool when the
water is stirred up; while I am on my way, someone
else gets down there before me."

~John 5:7

Bring to the Waters

No one comes to Baptism unless another brings him or
her. Maybe you were carried in your mother's arms, or in
later life a Christian friend walked with you to the healing waters of the Church where the Lord Jesus baptizes
us into his new life. With the grace of God our hearts are
changed, and we move from an unloving to a loving person, from isolation into community with God. We have
been enabled to pick up our mat of paralysis and to walk
into a God-immersed freedom of heart and soul to love
as we have been loved. The paralytic in today's gospel

was ill for thirty-eight years, and he was still waiting for someone to help him come to salvation. It is never too late for us or too late for us to help another. In this time and place, we are the hands and feet of the Lord Jesus. We are called to bring those we see paralyzed at heart to Jesus, so that they may walk with us into the kingdom of God. Most conversions stem from the example of someone who lives the Christian life with faith and love, and someone watching them exclaims, "I want to live like that. I want to give of myself as I see being given to me."

ACT

Today, I will think of someone I want to invite to come to church with me and formulate a plan to do so. An encouraging word or a walk beside another may bring a person to the waters of life.

PRAY

God, our Father,
I believe that in giving us your Son, you have given us everything.
I put my life in your hands.

WEDNESDAY, MARCH 18
FOURTH WEEK OF LENT

BEGIN

Seek a center of stillness surrounded by silence.
God will illumine your mind and enkindle your heart.

PRAY

Lord, in your great love, answer my plea for help.

LISTEN

Read John 5:17–30.

"Amen, amen I say to you, the Son cannot do anything on his own, but only what he sees the Father doing; for what he does, the Son will do also."

~John 5:19

Like Father, Like Son

In today's gospel, Jesus claims he is doing only what his Father is doing. They are one God, and to see Jesus is to see the Father. You ask, "What is the Father doing?" In the Creed we profess our belief in the "Father Almighty." We believe that God is love that is power and power that is love—not one or the other, but both love that is powerful and power that is loving. One without the other will not save us.

Because God is spirit, he acts as spirit in the world. God illumines minds to see the truth and enkindles hearts to embrace the good and love it well. Jesus walked among us and he healed the bodies of the sick. He meant that healing to be a sign pointing to the deeper healing it would generate. Jesus would bring us to faith in the Father and love for the ways of God in the world. The Father and the Son work hand-in-hand to illumine minds and enkindle hearts. Not everyone is told, "take up your mat and walk," but everyone is invited to share in the greatest miracle on earth, which is the conversion of human beings from unloving to loving and from untrusting to trusting.

ACT

Today, I will keep before me this question: Does "God, the Father Almighty" suggest power without love, or do we see the love of Jesus as the true face of God?

PRAY

God, our Father,
I believe that in giving us your Son, you have given us everything.
I put my life in your hands.

THURSDAY, MARCH 19
FOURTH WEEK OF LENT

BEGIN

Seek a center of stillness surrounded by silence.
God will illumine your mind and enkindle your heart.

PRAY

Loving God, may my life reveal your great love to all
I meet this day.

LISTEN

Read John 5:31–47.

"How can you believe, when you accept praise from
one another and do not seek the praise that comes
from the only God"?

~John 5:44

The Terrain Trumps the Map

Long before map-making was accomplished by satellites
in the sky, maps were made by folks who travelled the
terrain. Revisions were offered by those who knew the
lay of the land. Jesus accuses the religious leaders of his
day of searching the scriptures as a way to postpone an
encounter with the living embodiment of the heart of
the scriptures—himself, the real "terrain." They did not
want to come to Jesus in order to have life. So instead
they hid in the study of the scriptures, where they could
cherry-pick isolated texts to prove most anything conve-
nient to their conscience. We should remember that our
faith remains an encounter with the person, Jesus, and
not a study of words alone.

Long before the Christian scriptures were written
down, there were many baptized Christians living and

dying in their faith and love of Jesus Christ. They had yet to make the maps, but they were walking the terrain. The gospels were written by a community that was living the life of Christ, and the writing they produced came out of their experience. The scriptures were written by people of faith and love for others who wanted to learn from God and increase their faith and love. "Where your treasure is, there also is your heart."

ACT

I will ask myself, "Do I not only know my Christian faith, but live it? How can I more consistently put my hand in the hand of Jesus to walk with him into the future?"

PRAY

God, our Father,
I believe that in giving us your Son, you have given us everything.
I put my life in your hands.

FRIDAY, MARCH 20
FOURTH WEEK OF LENT

BEGIN

Seek a center of stillness surrounded by silence.
God will illumine your mind and enkindle your heart.

PRAY

Father, font of all life, you understand my weakness.
Help me to accept your hand and so to walk in your
ways.

LISTEN

Read John 7:1–2, 10, 25–30.

"Is he not the one they are trying to kill? And look, he
is speaking openly and they say nothing to him."

~John 7:25–26

Ripeness Is All

Jesus "did not wish to travel in Judea, because the Jews
were trying to kill him." He had taken over John the
Baptist's mission to call for repentance and conversion
of heart, because the kingdom of God was at hand. Jesus
knew that what happened to John and to the prophets
before John surely awaited him in Jerusalem. Nonetheless, he would serve the truth of his mission rather than
preserve his life. For a time, he continued his success-
ful ministry in Galilee, where he was well received. He
waited until the time was ripe. Before that point, his
hour had not come. We also need such discernment and
patience. Maybe your children or family seem to have
wandered far from God or from the Church, and maybe
we should recognize that their hour has not yet come.
God will wait for us, and God's providence is sovereign.

Everyone will have their own hour. God is not finished with us yet, and God's resources are beyond compare. We may think that it is easy to outrun the love of God, but we may all be surprised that God never tires of pursuing his children, and that God's loving patience is far greater than ours.

ACT

What good deed in my life am I postponing? I will name it and tame it!

PRAY

God, our Father,
I believe that in giving us your Son, you have given us everything.
I put my life in your hands.

Saturday, March 21
Fourth Week of Lent

BEGIN

Seek a center of stillness surrounded by silence.
God will illumine your mind and enkindle your heart.

PRAY

Lord God, on my own I can do nothing. In your
mercy, sustain me in doing what is good.

LISTEN

Read John 7:40–53.

Nicodemus, one of their members who had come to
him earlier, said to them, "Does our law condemn a
man before it first hears him and finds out what he is
doing?"

~John 7:50–51

Your God May Be Too Small

In our gospel reading today, Nicodemus tries to save
Jesus from a prejudicial condemnation, a verdict ren-
dered before due consideration. "The verdict first and
then the evidence," says the Red Queen of *Alice in Won-
derland*. So often the outcome is rigged in courts with
political bias. Do we judge God in the same irrational
way? Do we conjure up a picture of God unworthy of
the name and then decide we do not believe in such an
unbelievable God? Do we try to see God in the best light
and with the best theology, or have we already decided
that God is hard to please and then allow that prejudice
to justify our cool distance from the Divinity?

"Your God may be too small" is what I want to say.
That diminution of God may seem, and only seem, to

justify your distance. Everyone has a picture of God in their mind, whether it is ever spoken or not. You cannot avoid meaning something when you say the word "God." The only question is whether your theology of God is ample or cramped, more right or more wrong. We can do better, play fairer, and come closer to the truth about God, whose love and mercy are infinite.

ACT

Today, I will consider what I believe about God and whether what I believe keeps me skeptical. Do I consider opinions from many sides in any important life issue, such as how to describe God? Am I too quick to judge?

PRAY

God, our Father,
I believe that in giving us your Son, you have given us everything.
I put my life in your hands.

SUNDAY, MARCH 22
FIFTH WEEK OF LENT

BEGIN

Seek a center of stillness surrounded by silence.
God will illumine your mind and enkindle your heart.

PRAY

Father, conform me to the image of your son, who so
loved the world that he gave his life so that we might
live. May I follow his holy example this day and
always.

LISTEN

Read John 12:20–33.

"Whoever loves his life loses it, and whoever hates
his life in this world will preserve it for eternal life."

~John 12:25

Many Paradoxes

Philip is the intermediary of this Sunday's gospel. Some
Greeks who came to worship at the Passover feast ask
Philip to see Jesus. He brings them to Jesus. Nothing
more. It may be all that we are supposed to do. We do
not save others. We bring them to Jesus. They may ask
us to see Jesus, to explain to them why we live the way
we do. They may ask if they could also have something
of the joy and purpose they see in our way of living.
They are not asking to be like us in all things. They have
caught in our life a glimpse of Jesus. They have heard a
rumor in our talk of the wisdom of Jesus. They are not
asking to see more of us, but are asking us to take them
to see Jesus.

It is a delicate vocation to bring others to Jesus. We have to step aside. They will have to hear the paradoxes of the Gospel. More is less; losing one's life is finding it; the last shall be first; giving one's life is receiving it. We do not bring anyone to faith. Only Jesus does that, but we can be like Philip. We can bring our friends and acquaintances to where Jesus can be heard in the gospels and in our churches.

ACT

Who brought me to see Jesus? Have I thanked them? I will do so today, in conversation or via a note or in a prayer of thanksgiving. I will be on the lookout for anyone who might approach me to bring them to Jesus.

PRAY

God, our Father,
I believe that in giving us your Son, you have given us everything.
I put my life in your hands.

Monday, March 23
Fifth Week of Lent

BEGIN

Seek a center of stillness surrounded by silence.
God will illumine your mind and enkindle your heart.

PRAY

Father of mercy, let my former life slip away, and
a new life of race root me firmly in your kingdom
forever.

LISTEN

Read John 8:1–11.

"Let the one among you who is without sin be the
first to throw a stone at her."

~*John 8:7*

Saving Everyone

This tender story has a long history. It was not always
found in earlier manuscripts. Clearly the Christian
community, who in the end selected the scriptures that
would later become the canonical texts of the Bible,
insisted that this story rang true to their memory of Jesus
and that it must be included in the Bible. Jesus defended
women many times over in an age when women had
little defense. The men in the story drag her out in pub-
lic, no doubt without any cover for the occasion, and no
male accomplice in sight. Jesus writes on the ground.
He doodles, I think, too embarrassed to look up or to
say anything. When cornered by his opponents with a
demand for a verdict, he straightens up and reminds
them that they themselves are not without sin. No one
casts the first stone.

Jesus was not trying to embarrass the men and sock it to them for their hypocrisy. We might feel he should have been. More likely Jesus was trying to deter the men from a cruel violence that they would perhaps sorely regret the next day. In his merciful love, Jesus saved the woman and the men, too.

ACT

Do I ever visit or write to anyone in prison? Do I support prison reform? Do I take joy in the severe punishment of criminals or find sadness in human life so rough on everyone, innocent and guilty alike?

PRAY

God, our Father,
I believe that in giving us your Son, you have given us everything.
I put my life in your hands.

TUESDAY, MARCH 24
FIFTH WEEK OF LENT

BEGIN

Seek a center of stillness surrounded by silence.
God will illumine your mind and enkindle your heart.

PRAY

O Lord, hear my prayer, and let my cry come to you.
Hide not your face from me in the day of my distress.

~Psalm 102:2–3

LISTEN

Read John 8:21–30.

"When you lift up the Son of Man, then you will
realize that I AM."

~John 8:28

Calvary and Easter Morning

"When you lift up the Son of Man, then you will realize
that I AM." Could it be that the resurrection of Jesus from
the dead took place at the moment he died? We know
the women who came to the tomb on Sunday morning
found the tomb empty, but no one saw the tomb open
and Jesus rise from the dead on Easter morning. The rock
was rolled back so that the women could see into the
tomb, not so that Jesus could escape from the tomb. The
angel at the tomb said to the women, "Why are you looking for Jesus here? He is not here. He is risen." When,
how, where—we do not know. I AM is in capital letters
in our lectionary because that claim of Jesus echoes the
revelation of God to Moses at the burning bush. God did
not need time to think about raising Jesus. We needed
three days to believe that he really was dead. Jesus may

well have been raised from the dead at the moment of his death on the cross, at the moment of his being lifted up, exalted both in his love-filled dying and in his life-giving rising. We need more time, and the rock rolled back, to believe that he rose from the dead. I AM.

ACT

Today, I will think about why I hang a cross in my home or around my neck. Is it a decoration or a sign of grief and astonishment at God's prodigal love for us? Next time I make the sign of the cross, I will be mindful of the greatness of God's love for me.

PRAY

God, our Father,
I believe that in giving us your Son, you have given us everything.
I put my life in your hands.

Wednesday, March 25
Fifth Week of Lent

BEGIN

Seek a center of stillness surrounded by silence.
God will illumine your mind and enkindle your heart.

PRAY

Merciful Father, I ask your forgiveness. I am sorry
for all my sins. Illumine my mind grown dark and
enkindle my heart where it has grown cold.

LISTEN

Read John 8:31–42.

"If you remain in my word you will truly be my
disciples,
and you will know the truth, and the truth will set
you free."

~John 8:31–32

Sin Is Nonsense

Sin never made anyone free or truly happy. Sin enslaves
us, misleads us, confuses us, and leaves us with empty
promises, more alone and unhappy than before we
sinned. St. Augustine and St. Thomas Aquinas thought
of sin as an absence, as a privation of a good that should
be there, as a kind of nothingness or vacuum in the
world where whatever truly is remains truly good. Sin
is an illusion of the good. Reality is always good. Sin
is unreal, a love that is missing in action. Theology in
the main has found sin to be unintelligible. It makes no
sense. Sin is nonsense.

   If you seek happiness, and a life of virtue is the
train to any and all human happiness, it makes no sense

to get on the train to self-misery and harm to others. That is sin. That is non-sense, just plain old nonsense. The gospel today promises that "the truth will set you free," and the reason is simple: the truth makes sense. People who live a life of virtue rather than a life of sin live in the truth that makes sense and makes for that measure of happiness possible in this world of light and darkness.

ACT

Do I envy the glamorous life of people who have profited from taking advantage of others, whether in personal life or in economic life? Today, I will pray for their deliverance from sin and for my deliverance from envy of them.

PRAY

God, our Father,
I believe that in giving us your Son, you have given us everything.
I put my life in your hands.

THURSDAY, MARCH 26
FIFTH WEEK OF LENT

BEGIN

Seek a center of stillness surrounded by silence.
God will illumine your mind and enkindle your heart.

PRAY

Lord God, draw near. Deliver me from sin and help
me to live a fully Christian life that will lead me to the
glory of heaven.

LISTEN

Read John 8:51–59.

"Amen, amen, I say to you, whoever keeps my word
will never see death."

~John 8:51

For Whom the Bell Tolls

We often speak of life after death, but perhaps we should
say that Christians believe that we are given even now
a life that can go through death. Our body will die, but
our spirit in union with the Holy Spirit will live through
the death of this world. "Whoever keeps my word will
never see death." Surely this promise is a foreshadow-
ing of the Paschal Mystery we are about to celebrate at
Easter time. We may wonder if it could be true that we
will never see death. People may view the cemeteries
of the world and hesitate to believe that the souls of the
faithful departed, who to all appearances really died,
never saw death. Does the resurrection of the body take
place only on the last day? Might it be in the Eucharist
that we should put our hope of a life capable of going
through death? We hope not only in life after death, but

in the Eucharist we are joined to the life of Jesus whose body we receive and so pass through death with him. "This is the bread that came down from heaven, not like that which your ancestors ate, and they died. But the one who eats this bread will live forever" (Jn 6:58).

ACT

Am I afraid to die? What should I do? Perhaps I should take up the *Catechism of the Catholic Church* and see what hope it offers, together with the gospels.

PRAY

God, our Father,
I believe that in giving us your Son, you have given us everything.
I put my life in your hands.

Friday, March 27
Fifth Week of Lent

BEGIN

Seek a center of stillness surrounded by silence.
God will illumine your mind and enkindle your heart.

PRAY

In my distress I called upon the Lord and cried out to
my God;
From his temple he heard my voice, and my cry to
him reached his ears.

~Psalm 18:7

LISTEN

Read John 10:31–42.

"John performed no sign, but everything John said
about this man was true."

~John 10:41

No Good Deed Goes Unpunished

We may end up despising someone who does us a good
turn, precisely because we see that person as better than
we are. We resent the humiliating knowledge that we do
not do much good for others who cannot repay us. Jesus
died because goodness is strangely and frequently found
threatening and hurtful. A strong light reveals how poor
in virtue we are. A generous heart reminds us how stingy
our response to the needs of others remains. Jesus did
not die because of the accusation of blasphemy, which
was largely a cosmetic excuse on the part of his persecu-
tors. Jesus died because he suggested that the ordinary
folk, the poor and the burdened, should be freed from
the bad deal imposed on them in the name of the state

religion of Israel. Pilate was more honest in his condemnation of Jesus. He feared that he would be turned in to the authorities in Rome for not taking a stand against Jesus, whose teachings did not foster allegiance to Rome for the people who belonged first and foremost to God. Human beings are not to be exploited for political or economic reasons, and this message of Jesus alienated both the Roman worldly authority and the Jewish religious authority.

ACT

If asked why Jesus died, what would I say in twenty words or less? Think about it. Does it have any resonance with our own times? In what ways?

PRAY

God, our Father,
I believe that in giving us your Son, you have given us everything.
I put my life in your hands.

SATURDAY, MARCH 28
FIFTH WEEK OF LENT

BEGIN

Seek a center of stillness surrounded by silence.
God will illumine your mind and enkindle your heart.

PRAY

Lord God, you are ever at work in our souls, and you
gather your children to yourself. Bless those about to
be baptized and renew all the people of your Church.

LISTEN

Read John 11:45–56.

"What are we going to do?"

~John 11:47

Expedience

In today's gospel, it may sound like Jesus is a religious
rebel and the Jewish religious leaders want him elimi-
nated for the common good of the Jewish people. Better that one man die than the whole community perish.
More likely is this consideration: The religious leaders
kept their post and their income because, to keep peace,
the Romans needed them and, to stay in power, the Jewish leaders needed the Romans. Peace at any price. It was
a cozy relationship with the "occupation" and a mutu-
ally advantageous collaboration. The Romans saw Jesus
as a potential radical who could gather a huge crowd to
cheer his triumphal entry into Jerusalem. Not good. The
Roman garrison was vastly out-numbered in Jerusalem,
especially at the time of the festivals when the city was
over-crowded with pilgrims. Jesus was always truth-tell-
ing, as Christianity should be. He was a challenge for

everyone and, for some, a threat they feared. He spoke truth to power. People loved him, and they might well follow him. Better to take him out. Caiaphas said it succinctly: "You know nothing, nor do you consider that it is better for you that one man should die instead of the people, so that the whole nation may not perish" (Jn 11:49–50).

ACT

Do I vote for expedience and for my own interests rather than for justice and for the common good? Might I rethink what I support and how it impacts others?

PRAY

God, our Father,
I believe that in giving us your Son, you have given us everything.
I put my life in your hands.

MARCH 29

PALM SUNDAY OF THE LORD'S PASSION

BEGIN

Seek a center of stillness surrounded by silence.
God will illumine your mind and enkindle your heart.

PRAY

This is the day when our Lord and King came humbly into Jerusalem in order to lead us with him into the everlasting New Jerusalem. May I walk near to him today and all throughout this week.

LISTEN

Read Mark 11:1–10 and 14:1–15:47.

"Blessed is he who comes in the name of the Lord."

~Mark 11:10

From Palms to Nails

We may remember the first inauguration of President Obama and his walk up Pennsylvania Avenue to the White House. Crowds were lining the roadway and shouting out their greetings to the chief of state on his way to his presidential office. Jesus, hailed as the Messiah and recognized even by Pontius Pilate as "Jesus of Nazareth, King of the Jews," came riding into the capital city of Jerusalem as a meek and humble Savior of his people. The crowds shouted "Hosanna" and they threw down their clothes and palm branches to give Jesus the red-carpet treatment as he rode into his Messianic destiny. I can imagine Pope Francis chugging along in his Ford Focus on the *Via della Conciliazione* into the Vatican on his way to the throne of Peter, Bishop of Rome and Vicar of Christ the King. In Mark's passion story, which is read today as the gospel during Mass, we have an anointing of Jesus by an unknown woman, who pours precious ointment on his head, the ritual for anointing a king—a king who is about to enter into the last days of his life. Jesus then speaks words heard around the world. "Let her alone. . . . She has done what she could. She has anticipated anointing my body for burial. Amen I say to you, wherever the Gospel is proclaimed in the whole world, what she has done will be told in memory of her" (Mk 14:6–9).

ACT

Today, or at least before Holy Thursday, I will read the whole of Mark's passion narrative in one sitting. What touches me in the story this year?

PRAY

God, our Father,
I believe that in giving us your Son, you have given us everything.
I put my life in your hands.

MONDAY, MARCH 30
HOLY WEEK

BEGIN

Seek a center of stillness surrounded by silence.
God will illumine your mind and enkindle your heart.

PRAY

The Lord is my light and my salvation; whom should
I fear?
The Lord is my refuge; of whom should I be afraid?

~Psalm 27:1

LISTEN

Read John 12:1–11.

"You always have the poor with you, but you do not
always have me."

~John 12:8

Love Is Priceless

Today's gospel tells the story of Mary of Bethany, sister of
Lazarus and Martha, who anoints the feet of Jesus with
costly perfume. Like the unknown woman in yesterday's
gospel reading from Mark, there is an objection that the
money paid for the ointment should have been given to
the poor. Jesus replies that the poor will always be with
us; there will be no end of opportunities to serve them.
But this moment is special. The anointing of his feet by
Mary and of his head by the unnamed woman are recognized as a priceless anointing of his body before it is
beaten and crucified unto death. If we sold all the gold
wedding rings of the world, we could feed the poor for
many weeks.

We know that love is priceless and that even poor people want to give something precious to the one whom they love. There is a third story in Luke of an unnamed woman who washes the feet of Jesus with her tears and dries them with her hair. Whether it is one story told three ways, or three stories and three different women, we know that somebody loved Jesus to death before his enemies put him to death. We should take the stories to heart. You cannot love too much.

ACT

Why do I respond with love in the way that I do?
Have I thought much about it? To whom in my life do
I feel most free to show my love? Why do I limit love?

PRAY

God, our Father,
I believe that in giving us your Son, you have given
us everything.
I put my life in your hands.

TUESDAY, MARCH 31
HOLY WEEK

BEGIN

Seek a center of stillness surrounded by silence.
God will illumine your mind and enkindle your heart.

PRAY

Father of mercy, may I know your forgiveness and
love as we draw closer to the passion and death of
Jesus Christ.

LISTEN

Read John 13:21–33, 36–38.

"Amen, amen, I say to you, one of you will betray
me."

~John 13:21

Surely It Is Not I, Lord?

If you were the Roman governor of Jerusalem, or if you
were among the religious leaders in power at the good
will of the Roman governor Pontius Pilate, what might
you be thinking if a radical preacher rode triumphantly
into the city? Jesus was cheered on by enormous crowds
who overran the capital city at the time of the paschal
festival, and who were not happy with the foreign occupation of Jerusalem. Was Jesus the spark that would
ignite the revolution to free Israel? After all, he talked
of nothing but freedom from slavery of every kind. The
only group that Jesus never criticized was the Zealots,
who were actively trying to cast off Roman rule. In fact,
he chose Simon the Zealot as one of his apostles.

Then there was Judas, who was likely a cryptic
Zealot, hoping to light the fire of a mob in Jerusalem in

order to overthrow the Romans. If Jesus were arrested, Judas may have reasoned, he would either break out—after all, he worked miracles of every kind—or the crowds would rush the jail. The Romans would be greatly outnumbered. The plan, however, went badly. Judas may not have intended the death of Jesus. He returned the money and in self-punishment hanged himself. We don't know the whole story—do we need Judas to be very bad so that we can feel better?

ACT

Do I need others to be worse than I am so that I can feel better than I am? Do I put others down so that I can raise myself up? Today, I will name one person I tend to put down and decide on a way to break that habit.

PRAY

God, our Father,
I believe that in giving us your Son, you have given us everything.
I put my life in your hands.

WEDNESDAY, APRIL 1
HOLY WEEK

BEGIN

Seek a center of stillness surrounded by silence.
God will illumine your mind and enkindle your heart.

PRAY

God of tender compassion, protect me from sinful
temptation this day.

LISTEN

Read Matthew 26:14–25.

"What are you willing to give me if I hand him over
to you?"

~Matthew 26:15

What We Do and Why We Do It

In yesterday's meditation, we tried to understand the
Judas story without rushing to judgment that he was the
worst person on earth. One is suspicious that Judas has
become the scapegoat for all our sins, the person so bad
that all of us look good in comparison. The temptation to
pile on is almost irresistible. What a scumbag for all time!

One might ask, why make the case that Judas was
something other than a total villain? The answer is,
because perhaps it is the truth. Consider that (1) Jesus
chose him, and Jesus could read the human heart, (2)
Jesus knew he was to be betrayed, and yet he did not
intervene to stop it and so save Judas, and (3) Judas
betrayed Jesus with a kiss, perhaps because he thought
his plot to spark a revolution would succeed. As with
many a practical joke, we know that things can go ter-
ribly wrong. Perhaps it was not supposed to end this

way; that Jesus was supposed to be set free and then all of Jerusalem with him. Was that why Judas returned the money to the religious leaders, because, after all, it was not about the money—a sum that was large enough to be a plausible bribe and small enough to be a cheap bargain? In his remorse, Judas thought his own death was the only fitting punishment for the death of an innocent man that he had set in motion.

ACT

When others do me harm, do I ever consider that they may not have intended it? Am I quick to mercy and slow to judgment? I will identify in prayer one individual who has harmed me and pray that I can forgive and be reconciled with him or her.

PRAY

God, our Father,
I believe that in giving us your Son, you have given us everything.
I put my life in your hands.

APRIL 2
HOLY THURSDAY

BEGIN

Seek a center of stillness surrounded by silence.
God will illumine your mind and enkindle your heart.

PRAY

Lord Jesus, teach me to bow down in service to those
in need. May the Eucharist strengthen me for the
work of your kingdom today and always.

LISTEN

Read John 13:1–15.

"If I, therefore, the master and teacher, have washed
your feet, you ought to wash one another's feet."

~John 13:14

We Are the Bread

Why do we bother in our Eucharistic celebration to gather
a family to bring the bread and wine in a procession up
the main aisle to the altar? Would it not be easier to have
the sacristan put the bread and wine on the altar and get
on with it? Not having a procession would deprive the
congregation of a reminder of the mystery of the Eucharist. The bread brought up to the altar stands in for us. We
want to give our life to God, but God does not require
that we open up a vein and bleed out. Temple sacrifice
substituted an animal of sacrifice for sinful humans.
Christian Eucharist substitutes bread—without which we
cannot live—for our lives given over to God. We would
not all fit on the altar. The bread and wine stand in for us.
There are two miracles in every Eucharistic celebration.
The bread and wine become the body and blood of Jesus,

his life given for us. "This is my body," says Jesus, which is to say, "This is me for you." The second miracle is that we change. Our hearts are softened and we are enabled to love. We come to wash each other's feet in charity and love in service, as Jesus at the Last Supper showed us how to do.

ACT

No one expects me to wash their feet. Today I will find one way to turn expectations upside down and reach out in loving service to someone not expecting it.

PRAY

God, our Father,
I believe that in giving us your Son, you have given us everything.
I put my life in your hands.

April 3
Good Friday

Seek a center of stillness surrounded by silence.
God will illumine your mind and enkindle your heart.

PRAY

Into your hands I commend my spirit;
you will redeem me, O Lord, O faithful God.

~Psalm 31:6

LISTEN

Read John 18:1–19:42.

"Woman, behold your son." Then he said to his disciple, "Behold, your mother."

~John 19:26–27

It Is Finished

What did Jesus finish? Might I suggest he finished the revelation to us of how much God loves us? If Jesus had died peacefully in his bed after many years of goodness given and received, we would have gospel stories, but we would not have known how deep and far went the love of God for us. Looking on the crucifixion now we know. It is finished, and so is our resistance to God finished in its very substance and root. Our human quarrel with God has two complaints. First, God is too powerful, and thus God easily appears threatening to us. He holds all the high cards and we resent him. Second, God is too rich, and thus God easily engenders envy in us. We are so poor. There is nothing we have that we have not been given. We are not self-sufficient, and we do not like being perpetually indebted from the beginning to the end of our lives. When we look on God in Jesus crucified, however, God does not look very powerful nailed to the cross, nor does God look very rich naked and bleeding to death. Now we know. God simply loves us. "Mother, this is your son." And "Son, this is your mother." We are all in it together now.

ACT

Today, I will attend the Good Friday liturgy or read the whole of the passion story from John's gospel. I will sit in quiet contemplation before the day is through and call to mind what stands out about the liturgy or the Passion story. What does Good Friday say to me about how we Christians are to live?

PRAY

God, our Father,
I believe that in giving us your Son, you have given us everything.
I put my life in your hands.

Nicholas Ayo, C.S.C.,—born in New Jersey and educated by Benedictine sisters and monks—is professor emeritus in the program of liberal studies at the University of Notre Dame. He has been a member of the Congregation of Holy Cross since 1953, he graduated from Notre Dame and Moreau Seminary in 1956, and he was ordained a Roman Catholic priest in 1959. After pursuing theological studies in Rome, Fr. Ayo studied literature at Duke University and taught at the University of Portland for ten years. His ministry assignments have included working with Holy Cross novices in Vermont and Colorado. He is an award-winning author of twelve books and numerous articles on Catholic spirituality and theology.